drum tuning
THE ULTIMATE GUIDE

by Scott Schroedl

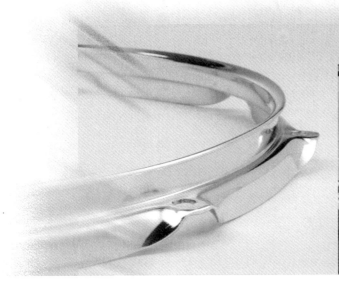

PLAYBACK+
Speed • Pitch • Balance • Loop

To access audio visit:
www.halleonard.com/mylibrary

Enter Code
6787-0553-7856-6433

ISBN: 978-0-634-03925-6

HAL•LEONARD®

Visit Hal Leonard Online at
www.halleonard.com

Contact Us:
Hal Leonard
7777 West Bluemound Road
Milwaukee, WI 53213
Email: info@halleonard.com

In Europe contact:
Hal Leonard Europe Limited
Distribution Centre, Newmarket Road
Bury St Edmunds, Suffolk, IP33 3YB
Email: info@halleonardeurope.com

In Australia contact:
Hal Leonard Australia Pty. Ltd.
4 Lentara Court
Cheltenham, Victoria, 3192 Australia
Email: info@halleonard.com.au

drum tuning
THE ULTIMATE GUIDE

TABLE OF CONTENTS

ACKNOWLEDGMENTS

Special thanks goes out to the following people for helping me to make music my life: My wife, Melyssa, for her inspiration, friendship, love, and constant support in my life and musical endeavors; my parents, Ed and Jean Schroedl, for allowing me to practice the loudest instrument whenever I wanted to while growing up in their house; my first drum teacher, Evan Fisher, for inspiring me to always play my best; all of the musicians I've had the pleasure to play with over the years; my students, past and present, for allowing me to shape their musical minds; Roy Burns and Chris Brady at Aquarian Drumheads; Darrell Johnston at Axis Pedals; Ed Clift, Steve Riskin, and Rich Mangicaro at Paiste Cymbals; Jay Jones at Noble & Cooley Drums; Dick Smith at Midco International; Vic Firth, Neil Larrivee, Mike Hoff, and Rick Drumm at Vic Firth Drumsticks; TJ Martin at Ddrum; Brent King; Brent "Jr." Peterson; and everyone at Hal Leonard Corporation.

Extra special thanks to Aquarian Accessories for supplying the drumheads used for the recordings and photos of this book.

Drum set tuning has been a frustrating process for many drummers over the years. There are about as many different tuning techniques as there are drummers. Tuning becomes very personal, and gives drummers their own particular sound and style. Let's face it; guitarists have it easy. They're able to plug an electric guitar into a tuner and make adjustments while referencing the pitch on the readout. They only have one tuning mechanism per string. Drum tuning is much more difficult and challenging. There are many overtones associated with the overall "pitch" of a drum. Tuning a drum is all about recognizing these differences in pitch. Drums use anywhere from five to ten tension rods to tune one head—and most drums use two heads!

This book has been designed as an easy step-by-step guide for the beginner, but can also be used by professionals who want to get the most out of their drums. Some of the techniques described within may seem difficult to understand—and hear—at first; but by focusing on the basics of tuning, will come to you in time. You will find *your* signature sound through better tuning. Not only will you learn how to tune your drums, you'll also learn how to prepare and change heads systematically. Drum tuning is very subjective, and it ultimately comes down to personal taste. You will be shown which tuning techniques to use to achieve better sounds, but *how* you use them is up to you. The best way to get better at tuning (or anything, for that matter) is to practice—a lot! I had many great opportunities to practice tuning with drums differing in brand and quality when I worked for several years at a drum shop.

Well-tuned drums not only sound better, they are more satisfying to play. As you begin to fine-tune your ears to the subtleties of better tuning, you'll start to notice great differences in sounds—due not only to drum quality, but also to the different shell materials. Although you will be able to tune your drums many different ways, the size (diameter and length), shell material, and construction will ultimately determine the sound and range that your drum is capable of producing. Buy the best drums you can afford, or the quality to match your situation. Obviously, if you only plan to play in your basement for your own enjoyment, you won't necessarily need a professional drum set like a studio session drummer would. Just be aware of what you should expect out of your drums. With less expensive drums, you'll get to a point where it just won't sound any better; and because lesser-quality drums have a limited range, it may take less time to tune them. High-end drums of good quality will mechanically tune with ease; but it can sometimes take more time to get to know their every nuance, since the possibilities of tone and tuning range are so much greater.

It is best to read this book in its entirety from the beginning instead of skipping around, since many things talked about later in the book may refer back to things mentioned earlier. You may even change your mind about the types of heads or muffling you'll use, or the tools you'll need to complete the tuning process contained within.

For starters, the best (and least frustrating) way to learn tuning is to practice with new drumheads. Old, worn out drumheads have been beaten, pulled, and stretched so much that you may never get them to sound good—no matter how great you are at tuning. So, give yourself a break and buy new heads! Although it's very educational to try different types of heads and combinations in order to practice tuning, it's best not to buy a matching set for your toms until you're sure that they'll work for your musical situation. You may even want to start out by buying two single-ply tom heads on which to practice the tuning techniques contained within before buying a whole set of heads. If you have a 12" tom, this would be a good choice to practice on. You may decide to use different heads on your set as a whole later, but these heads are great for learning to tune.

Generally speaking, you can figure on spending about a dollar per inch-diameter per drumhead. Remember—just because the bottom heads aren't hit doesn't mean they don't wear out. Every time you hit the top head, the air inside the drum also pushes and stretches the bottom head, helping to produce the drum's overall tone; so if it's been a few years, you may want to change them too. Incidentally, the bottom heads are one of the most overlooked and misunderstood parts of the drum tuning process.

You will first need to figure out what size of heads you'll need. You will need to measure the diameter of each drum *inside* the hoop.

What you will actually measure here is the drum shell. Just to give you an idea of drum diameters, a typical, five-piece drum set consists of a 22" bass drum, a 14" snare, and 12", 13", and 16" toms. The measurements should always be rounded to the nearest inch. If you are not sure of the size, take your old drumheads with you when buying new ones, and have a salesperson help you, just to be safe. Don't toss the old heads out yet; I'll give you a useful tip for using them later.

Lug Spring Rattle

Since your old heads are still on the drums, it's a good time to check for spring rattle within the lugs. Most mid- and high-end drums today use either self-aligning lugs with nylon inserts, or lugs that are tapped and threaded with no swivel nut.

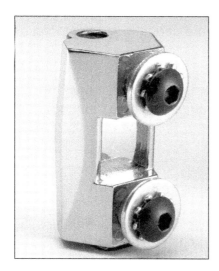

A third type of lug has a spring inside. Many of the older or more inexpensive drums are likely to get a rattling sound from these springs.

This problem is most discouraging when in a recording session, since most drum recordings of today include the practice of close miking. You may want to remove the cymbals from your drum set in order to more clearly hear your drums and listen for lug rattle. Sometimes, you may be fooled by rattles that are not due to lugs—such as the sound of a washer on a loose tension rod, or the spiked end of bass drum spurs with retractable rubber feet. If you are using the spiked end, make sure to thread the rubber end all the way back, so that it's tight and won't rattle.

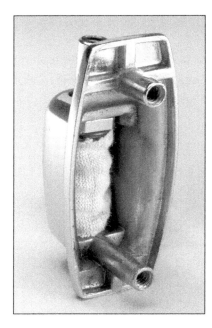

If you do detect a rattle coming from a lug, you can quiet the noise by packing it. The best way to do this is to wrap the spring with either felt or cotton cloth. First, remove the heads and all of the lugs. *Carefully* remove the spring (it's under tension, and might shoot out) from the lug. Cut felt or cotton cloth so that it wraps around the spring, covering the width of the space within the lug where the spring sits, keeping in mind that when the spring is not compressed inside the lug, it's longer.

Replace the lug on the drum and tighten it back on. Be sure not to over-tighten, as that could break the lug.

Just in case, you may as well pack all of your drums' lugs to avoid future problems. Nothing is more disheartening in a recording session than when you think all of your drums are tuned and you're ready to go, and then the engineer hears a rattle from your drums—and you spend an hour trying to find it.

Tools for the Job

To begin tuning, you'll need some essential tools. For the very basics, a drum key and drumstick will do the trick. To make the job easier, and to do some important maintenance, you could use some extra things. There are special drum keys available that fit a drill or cordless screwdriver, and will make the removal the heads much quicker. After removing worn-out heads, a towel or vacuum will come in handy to clean the stick shavings at the hoop, and to dust the inside of the shell. A candle or bees wax is sometimes used on the shell's bearing edge. Typically, to tighten the lugs onto the shell, you'd need either a slotted or Phillips screwdriver; but occasionally, on certain brands, you'll instead need a specific-sized hex wrench. To lube the threaded inserts within the lugs, use light oil—even petroleum jelly will work in a pinch. Unless you are tuning your drums on a carpeted floor, a towel comes in handy for muting the drumhead you're not working on.

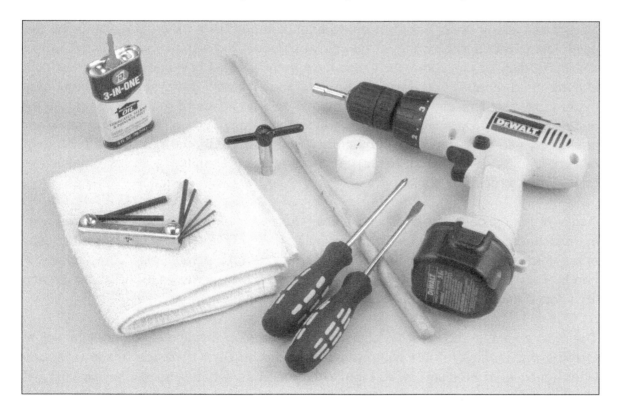

DRUMHEAD BASICS

Although many components contribute to the sound of a drum, the heads are its primary source of resonance. Drumheads come in many different sizes, thicknesses, textures, and in some cases, colors. Now that you have measured your drums and know the size of heads you need, you will also need to decide on the type.

There is no such thing as a "studio" drumhead. It is true that players sometimes use different heads in the studio versus live, but for different reasons. For example, the use of thicker heads will ensure the durability necessary to get through a live performance. It's all about the sound you are trying to achieve: open and resonant, or deep and muffled.

How to Decide on the Drumheads You Need

Think about the style of music you intend to play, and that will help you to determine the type of heads you need. Do you want to tune high and open for a tight jazz tuning that gives lots of rebound and ring, or do you want loose and slappy-sounding toms with a dead-sounding kick for rock? You'll also have to think about how you play—hard or light. Do you need durability or sensitivity on your snare drum? There are even drumheads made today that emulate the sound of the old calfskin heads of yesteryear, but with the durability of the plastics we've grown accustomed to today. Through drumhead choice and tuning, *your* sound is determined by the following factors: the drum's overall pitch (high or low), tone (dark, mellow, or bright), sustain (length of resonance), and articulation (the attack when struck with a stick).

Types of heads basically start with the amount of plies and/or thickness. Drumhead manufacturers measure ply thickness in mils (1/1000 of an inch). Due to their greater mass, thick heads require more force to be moved, and vibrate more slowly than thin heads. They also produce a lower overall pitch than thin heads do at the same tension. Thin heads are just the opposite: they sound bright and ring more freely.

TRACK 1

The most common and versatile heads are comprised of a single ply of medium weight. Listen to an example of this type of head's sound on Track 1. These heads work best when tuned from medium-low to high. When used as a batter head (the top side you play on), they have a quick stick response and produce a full sustaining tone. They have a medium life span compared to the other types discussed below. Used as a resonant head (the bottom side you don't play on), they project a full sustaining tone, and are a favorite among many players. These heads are what most manufacturers install on their new drums. Keep in mind that the heads that come stock on most new, inexpensive drum sets aren't nearly of the quality that you could buy as replacement heads. Therefore, if you replace them, your drums may sound even better than when you first bought them.

TRACK 2

If you are a heavy-hitter looking for a deadened, deeper tone with more attack, you may want to try two-ply heads on the batter side of your toms, snare, or bass drum. Two-ply heads come in two varieties; both types use two pieces of Mylar, but on one type the outer inch or so of the two plies is glued together, making its sounds more muffled. These types of heads work best when tuned low (on bass drum and toms)—almost to the point of wrinkling. Due to the actual mass of two-ply heads, both types tend to sound deeper, and put out less volume than single-ply heads. With two-ply heads you will get more attack, less sustain, and a longer playing lifespan. Listen to an example of this type of head's sound on Track 2. Although not recommended, you could use these heads on the resonant side of tom-toms. The sound will result in a deep "thud," with not much sustain or clarity.

TRACK 3

The third basic type is the single-ply, thin drumhead. These work great for lighter players who want more sensitivity and a more open or sustaining sound. The best tuning range for these heads would be from medium to high. When using this type as a batter head, you'll notice a quick stick response and a clear, resonant sound. Listen to Track 3 for an example of this. The trade-off is that heads of this type are less durable because they're thin. They'll also work great on the resonant side of the toms, but won't sound quite as full as a medium-weight, single-ply head.

The fourth type of head is one specifically designed for the snare side drumhead. It's much thinner than any batter head, and is designed to work in conjunction with the wire snares. These heads come in a few different, extremely thin thicknesses, and are used only as snare resonant heads.

It may be helpful to get drumhead product catalogs, visit your local drum shop, or visit the websites of different drumhead manufacturers to acquaint yourself with the many options available. They are always designing new methods of manufacturing, types of heads, and materials every year. The major drumhead manufacturers include Aquarian, Attack, Evans, and Remo. Some drum set manufacturers, such as Ludwig, Premier, and Sonor, also produce their own heads. It is also helpful to get opinions from your drum instructor, drum shop salesmen, and great local players; and to read drumming magazines with interviews of your favorite drummers for their head combinations and tuning tips. The point is, get more than one opinion. What your friend or favorite player uses may not work for you or your style. Gather as much information as you can, and determine what pertains to your particular style and sound.

Tom Head Configurations

For some different ideas on standard tom head combinations, you may want to try some of these choices:

TRACK 4

A single ply of medium weight on the top and bottom. Listen to Track 4 to hear an example of this sound. This combination works great for all-around playing. These also come in a white-coated version. These heads with this coating tend to sound slightly warmer and mellower than the clear-head versions. You could even put a coated head on top, and a clear one on the bottom. The major point here is that they should be of the same basic thickness.

TRACK 5

A double-ply on the top and a medium-weight, single-ply on the bottom. Listen to Track 5 to hear an example of these. The double-ply will give you more durability if you play hard, and give a "wet" sound to the attack. The two-ply batter head will also sound more muffled and deeper in general, and allow you to tune lower than with single-ply heads.

TRACK 6

If you are a light player who wants an open sound, try a single-ply of medium or thin weight on the top, and a single-ply of thin on the bottom. Listen to Track 6 to hear an example of these heads.

Whatever types of heads you decide on, you should be consistent in using the same type on all of the toms. For instance, if you decide on using a two-ply batter head, use them on all the toms, and make sure that they are all the same brand. Then, for the resonant side, you could use a medium, single-ply, and match the brand and thickness on all the tom bottoms. This will allow you to achieve a consistent sound between your toms.

Snare Head Configurations

Since you may be using only one snare drum on your set at a time, changing your head type or tuning will greatly change the overall sound of you drum set. Snare drums use very different types of heads on the top versus the bottom. The batter heads are really the same as those used on the toms, but many specialty snare batter heads are also available, which enhance the characteristic sounds of snare drums. The major difference with snare drums lies in the bottom snare drum head—better known as the snare side head. Although snare side heads can vary in thickness, they are much thinner than any batter head; and because of this, should never be hit with sticks (other than very light tapping while tuning). These heads are thin so that they form around the snare beds (discussed later), which allows the snares to vibrate against the snare side head—which gives it the actual snare drum sound.

Snare side heads are always single-ply, but vary in thickness. If you are a very light player, use the thinnest head for the greatest sensitivity. For all around general use, a medium thickness will work extremely well. If you play quite hard, you may want to use a thicker snare side head.

Snare drum batter heads are often the same as those used for toms, but some manufacturers offer specific heads for snare drums exclusively. A few examples include:

• Single-ply, either white-coated with a dot underneath, or clear with a dot on top. The dot adds slight muffling to a single-ply head, as well as durability. The dot is placed underneath the coated head so that it doesn't inhibit brush playing. Incidentally, the white coating was originally developed to give a rough texture to plastic heads, for the purpose "swooshing" brushes on them.

• Single-ply, white-coated with vent holes near the edge to make the sound more "dry."

• Some snare batters are made of other materials—such as Kevlar—for added strength and durability.

• Another type uses a loose muffling ring around the underside perimeter, which aids in decreasing sustain of the head.

The most common snare drum batter head is a single ply of medium weight with a white coating for added warmth, which also, because of its texture, is favorable for playing with brushes. For more durability and muffling, try a two-ply drumhead, or another of the specialty heads just mentioned. A two-ply head is also great for toning down some of the harshness associated with some of the metal shell snare drums.

You can get many different sounds out of a drum just by changing heads, but keep in mind that you may need more than one snare drum to achieve the many sounds represented in music today. Don't expect to get a deep, full, ballad sound out of a 3" x 13" piccolo snare. Know the drum's limitations.

Bass Drum Head Configurations

The bass drum is similar to the toms in that its resonant head has quite an effect on the overall resonance of the drum. Typically, drummers will use some sort of muffling to achieve their bass drum sound. Many bass drum heads now come with different types of built-in muffling. You, too, may want to use additional muffling, but the heads that are available today are a great place to start.

Bass Drum Batter Heads

Bass drum batter heads come in one- or two-ply configurations. Sometimes there may be more than one two-ply head available from the same manufacturer. This is because one of the two plies may be of a different thickness, so as to give variety to double-ply head sounds.

A double-ply head will increase durability, add slight muffling due to more mass, and give a more focused attack with a tight, low-end sound. A single-ply head will have a more open sound, be more sensitive, and have a smoother attack with lots of low end.

Bass Drum Resonant Heads

Resonant heads for bass drums are one-ply, but with some variations, such as those that include a removable control ring near the outer edge, or those that have dampening materials adhered to the head itself. Check the many options available from the different drumhead manufacturers before making your decision.

Resonant heads are also available with a pre-cut hole for the insertion of a microphone. This hole also helps to alleviate beater bounce-back, which occurs when air inside the drum cannot escape.

DRUM CONSTRUCTION
AND HEAD PROPERTIES

There are many variables that make up the overall sound of a drum: the type of shell material; the depth, diameter, and thickness of the shell; the number of lugs; type of hoop; type of head; the finish; the degree of cut used on the bearing edge; and the way the drum is mounted. Without getting too in-depth about drum construction, I'd like to give you some background information before we start learning to tune.

Shell Materials, Plies, and Depths

The high-end drum shells of today are made out of many different types of wood—with maple and birch still the most popular. Some manufacturers mix different types of wood within the different plies of the shell. Don't get hung up on "this drum has this many plies, and this one has that many plies." The most important thing is that your drums sound good to you. Some drum manufacturers will choose the number of shell plies based on the diameter of the drum. Thinner shells will vibrate more than thicker shells; they will sound deeper in pitch, and fuller, because the thin shell vibrates with the heads to generate its overall tone. A thicker shell tends to sound focused, shallower, and less full, and is more reliant on the heads to give the drum its tone. The purpose of the shell, more or less, is to support the heads. Thicker-shelled drums were popular in the '80s, and drum manufacturers, through advertising, made it almost seem more prestigious to have them. But then the trend began to lead toward thinner shells. Some drum manufacturers even offer high-end snare drums built out of one thick, single ply of maple, which vibrates more freely than shells made out of many thinner plies put together.

Some drum shells include a reinforcement ring at each end of the shell. This is used mostly to help support thinner shell designs; but it also adds mass to the shell, which raises the shell's natural pitch, and gives a more defined attack to the sound.

Materials other than wood are sometimes used to make drum shells. You'll see, mostly in snare drums, different materials such as brass, steel, bronze, and aluminum; but some manufacturers have used, for example, acrylic, aluminum, and carbon fiber for complete sets.

Shell depth options have increased over the years, and especially affect how deep a tom sounds, and how quickly it responds when hit. For example, years ago, a tom shell with a 12" diameter would've been 8" deep and considered the "standard" size. Since the top and bottom heads of such drums are fairly close together, the response when hitting it is quite quick. The same diameter drums with depths of either 10" or 11" are considered "power" sized toms. The deepest toms are called "square" sized toms, since the depth is the same as the diameter. Both power- and square-sized toms respond much more slowly, because the heads are much farther apart. In the late 1990s, yet another size became popular— the "fast," or "quick" sized toms. The depths of the fast/quick toms fall between the depths of the standard and power sizes, and respond somewhere between them as well.

Bearing Edges

The bearing edge is another very important factor in drum sound and tuning. The bearing edge is either end of the cylindrical drum shell the—only point at which the drumhead touches the shell.

The bearing edge must be perfectly true in order for the head to seat properly, and for the drum to be tuned to its full potential. Every time you change heads, check the condition of the bearing edges for nicks, divots, or rough spots. If you notice any irregularities, you can have these edges re-cut by a professional. There are two bearing edge cuts. The first, in modern drums, is typically a 45° chamfer cut on the inside bearing edge, which ensures the best trade-off between attack and overall tone. The second cut is a round-over cut, which is the outside cut of the bearing edge, located where the collar of the drumhead contacts the shell. Sometimes, this outside cut is also 45°, which increases sustain, as the sharper edge leaves less contact area with the head. Many vintage drum shells have nothing more than a wide, round-over cut, which produces less attack and sustain, and gives the impression of more overall warmth, because more area is touching the head.

Shell Interiors

The interior of a shell will also affect the tone. A shiny, or heavily lacquered, interior will produce a much brighter sound due to the reduced absorption of sound into the wood. In comparison, a rougher, or non-lacquered, interior will sound warmer because of its porous, sound-absorbing surface.

Shell Exteriors

Drum shell exteriors are available in many colors and patterns. Wood shells are available with a plastic covering, a lacquered finish, or are treated with oil. Most inexpensive drums come finished with a plastic covering, but some high-end drums use this too. The plastic will help the shell withstand scratches and minor bumps. Plastic-covered, high-end drums offer many exciting patterns for visual appeal. It has been argued, however, that the plastic covering inhibits the drum shell's natural vibration.

Plastic covering

Drums not covered in plastic are either finished with high-gloss lacquer, or rubbed with wood oil.

Lacquer finish

Finish rubbed with wood oil

Both of these options were available years ago in the high-end range only, but many manufacturers today offer limited lacquered colors on their mid-line sets, too. The more expensive drums are finished with a greater number of coats; the finish of which is comparable to that of fine furniture.

Hoops

A drum's hoops will affect its tuning, sound, and feel. Triple-flanged hoops are standard on most drums. They are made of steel, formed (bent) into shape, and welded.

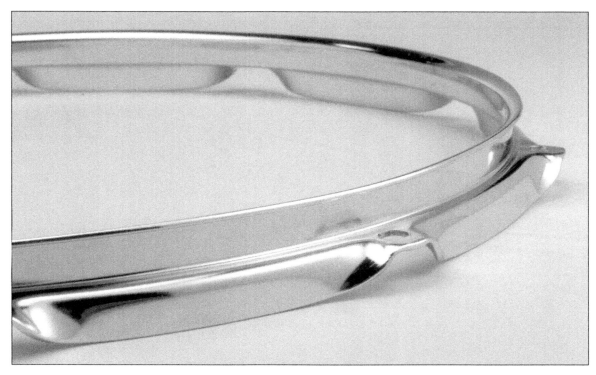

Triple-flanged hoop

Triple-flanged hoops can vary in thickness between manufacturers. They make hitting the drumhead more "giving" and "spongy-feeling," and can help disguise shell irregularities. When tuning, they are more forgiving, since they "give" slightly in relevance to the tension at each lug point. The thicker triple-flanged hoops can begin to take on die-cast hoop characteristics. Also, if your hoop is bent in any way, it will make tuning very difficult. You can either try bending it back to true, or replace it to get the most even tuning possible out of your drum.

Die-cast hoops are formed in a die and are very rigid.

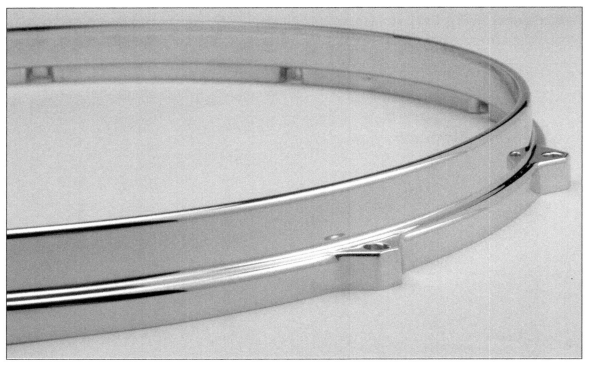

Die-cast hoop

TRACK 7

You will find these hoops on the more expensive snare drums and drum sets. Die-cast hoops have a feel that is quite the opposite of triple-flanged hoops. They make the drumhead feel much harder and more solid when hit in the center, and give a sharper attack to the sound. They also affect the overall tone of the drum. On toms, especially when tuned higher, they bring out a sort of "honk" quality; and in general, are less warm sounding. Listen to Track 7 for an example of this. On snare drums, they add more "crack" to rim shots, and make slamming backbeats feel much more solid. Track 8 demonstrates this. The tuning of drums with die-cast hoops requires much more precision, since there is virtually no give to them. Since they are more rigid, turning one tension rod also will affect the adjacent lugs, and even the whole head in general. These hoops can make tuning trickier at first, but definitely have an appealing quality to them.

TRACK 8

Wood hoops have traditionally been used on bass drums, but, to keep costs down, many of the less expensive sets now use metal hoops. Some drum companies even offer wooden hoops on toms and snare drums. The wood hoops generally have a warmer sound, since they absorb some vibration when the drum is struck.

Amount of Lugs

The number of lugs on a drum has an effect on how the drum tunes and sounds. To cut costs, beginner drum sets will use fewer lugs. But many high-end snare drums, which normally use as many as ten lugs, may use as few as six to create a different sound. The fewer lugs there are, the coarser the tuning, and the more complex the overtones—due to the lengthened distance between the lugs. The resulting sound, when fewer lugs are used, can be described as "darker," as there are less high frequencies. By designing smaller lugs, many drum manufacturers have reduced the amount of lug contact on the shell, which helps the drum shell resonate more easily.

Suspension Mounts

Prior to the '80s, tom mount brackets were always attached directly to the shell. Some even had the tom arms protruding through the shell. You may already know that the more mass attached to the shell, the less freely it will vibrate; and certainly, a hole in the shell can't be good for sustain, either. So, to bring out the drums' natural sustain, Gary Gauger invented a suspension system called Resonance Isolation Mounting System, or RIMS for short. This component allowed the tom mount bracket to be removed from the shell altogether, and attach instead to the RIMS unit, which suspended the drum through the tension rods—allowing the shell to resonate freely.

Many drum manufacturers now include their own versions of RIMS, mostly on their high-end drums; but retrofit mounts are available for use on any brand and quality of drums today.

The best place to begin to understand tuning is with the tom-toms. The process you'll learn is a systematic approach to changing all of your tom heads together as a group; but you may use the knowledge to work on only one drum at a time, if you desire.

Tom-toms (or toms) can range in size, typically from six to eighteen inches in diameter. They come in two varieties: single- or double-headed. Single-headed toms, also known as concert toms, produce a bright sound with minimal sustain. The sound of these drums stresses the attack rather than the tone. Double-headed toms are the most popular, and generate more warmth and sustain due to the additional vibrations of the second head. By using two heads, you gain better control of the tom's sustain through different tuning combinations.

The Tuning Process

Assuming you still have the old heads on your drums, and you've purchased new batter and resonant heads, begin by taking the toms off of your drum set. Place them with the resonant side up, in the order of size, on a carpeted floor. You must mute the heads you're not working on so that you can hear only the one being tuned. Another option is to set the drum you are tuning on a towel. You may want to double check that you do have all the correct new drumheads before removing the old ones.

Starting with the largest tom, remove the resonant head. Using a drum key or a drill with the drum key attachment, turn the tension rods counter-clockwise to remove the head. It's a good idea to turn each one just a little at a time, rather than loosening one completely and moving on to the next. This is especially true on snare drums, since they are usually tensioned very tightly to avoid uneven stress on the shell, head, and hoop. If you are not using a drill with the drum key attachment, try using two drum keys on opposite lugs to speed up the removal process. Once the tension rods are loose, you can spin them all the way out of the lug. You don't need to remove the tension rods from the hoop; just let them dangle as you pull the head and hoop off of the drum shell. It's handy to have your drum stool nearby on which to set the old head and hoop; the tension rods can just hang over the stool.

Now that the head is off of the drum, clean out any dust or debris that may have come in through the air vent and accumulated on the inside of the drum.

Take a moment to inspect the bearing edge (at the open end of the shell) by running your finger over it to detect any nicks or rough spots. It should feel uniform all the way around. Any irregularities, especially those that are severe, will ultimately affect the tuning and sound of your drum. You can also check the evenness of the bearing edge by removing both heads and placing the shell on a flat, level surface (such as a piece of granite). Aim a light inside the shell to see if any light escapes between the shell and granite. If so, you probably should have your bearing edges re-cut by a professional. It's best not to attempt anything of the sort on your own. If you find something like a slight rough spot, you could go ahead and lightly sand it to smooth it out. If you are not sure, have a professional look at it before you make it worse.

A way to reduce friction at the head and shell is to wax the bearing edge with beeswax or a candle (don't melt it). Rub it on sparingly, and run your finger over it to smooth it into the edge.

Tighten all of the screws that hold the lugs on the shell, being careful not to over-tighten. These screws tend to loosen up over time from vibration. You can also lubricate the threaded insert on the lug where the tension rod goes, if needed. Use a light oil or petroleum jelly to keep things moving freely.

Place the new drumhead, and spin it to make sure it doesn't bind in any way on the shell. If it does, your shell may be slightly out of round, or the head may be defective. More than likely, it's the shell; and if so, it's impossible to fix. If the head binds in a certain spot, spin it until you find a place where it doesn't, and leave it there. In the case of older drums, many of their shells were made slightly larger, and new heads may always bind. If the new heads don't bind on the drums, I prefer to align the logo on the head with the name badge on the drum. This way, I know where the front of the drum and the mount are, at a glance. I also like to have the head logo at the furthest point away from me (at twelve o'clock), when tuning the drum in front of me.

Now separate the hoop from the old head and clean any dust and stick shavings that may have accumulated there. Inspect the hoop to see if it is uneven in any way. If it is, you may want to try to bend it back, or just replace it. An uneven hoop will affect the tuning of your drum. Place the hoop onto the new head, which is already on the drum. Align the dangling tension rods with the lugs so that they'll pull straight through. It is very important that the head goes on straight. If there is any play between the drumhead and the shell, wiggle it back and forth until it is even on the shell. Now, being careful not to move the head, align the hoop on the head. This is especially crucial on entry-level drum sets—since manufacturers use less lugs, and the tolerances aren't as good, sometimes the head will slip out of the hoop if not aligned properly.

With your hands on opposite tension rods, finger-tighten them into the lugs, being careful not to cross-thread.

Do this until all of the tension rods are inserted into the lugs. Starting at the lug just to the right of the head logo, with one hand, press the hoop down lightly, and finger-tighten the rod again.

You will know it's tight enough when the washer no longer spins freely when touched. This also brings up a good point: Make sure you have washers between every tension rod and the hoop. These washers can be metal or nylon. I prefer using nylon. Many high-end drums come standard with nylon washers installed.

Next, press down on the hoop directly across from the first lug, and do the same thing. Use the lug order shown below.

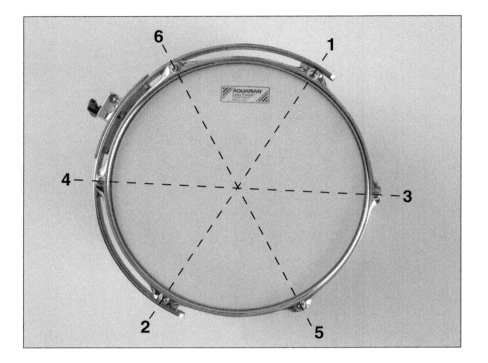

Once you finish this, go around one more time repeating this same procedure—just to make sure you are starting very evenly.

Using your drum key, and again, starting to the right of the head logo, turn each tension rod one half-turn. In order to be consistent, glance at your drum key's position before and after turning it to ensure you made a half-turn. Now tighten the opposite rod the in same way; then move to the next rod, just to the right of where you first started, and continue in the same fashion as shown in the photo above, until you've tightened each rod one half-turn. The reason for this gradual tightening, in this order, is to avoid pulling the head to one side. There are many opinions on the lug order to follow when tuning. It doesn't really matter much which pattern you follow, as long as you are tuning only a little at a time.

Seating the Head

This process stretches the Mylar drumhead over the bearing edge in order to "seat" it evenly on the drum, and forms the collar of the head for your particular drums. It also takes out any slack from the Mylar, which may initially slip.

Place your palm in the center of the drumhead, and put your other hand on top of it, as if you're giving CPR.

Press down fairly hard three or four times, to stretch the head a little (basically, so that the Mylar won't slip any more in its collar when you begin tuning). You may hear a cracking sound, due to the settling of the drumhead resin while doing this. Track 9 demonstrates this sound. This is normal. You won't really notice any cracking sound when using Aquarian heads, since they are locked in their hoop, 360° around, with no slippage (which makes our job easier when tuning!).

TRACK 9

Notice that after stretching the head, it may be lower in pitch. Tighten the head again until you begin to hear an actual tone, and continue doing so until you reach the general desired pitch. You will want to tension the head up enough to eliminate any wrinkles. Sometimes you may already be close, and it will only take the tightening up of one lug to get an initial tone from the head.

Fine-Tuning

At this point, I want to mention that you should be in a quiet environment in order to clearly hear the different pitches at each lug. With a drumstick, tap the head about one inch from the hoop at each lug point to hear differences in pitch.

TRACK 10 If at a few lugs you can only hear the start of a tone, slowly begin to tension up the others until you can hear the same thing. The object here is to get the tension even at each lug point, in order to give you the fullest tone and sustain possible for that drumhead. You may have found, if your drum is of a higher quality (with true bearing edges, consistent hoops), that you were very close already; especially since you also took the time to start at an even tension, and turned the drum key evenly. To fine-tune, find the lug with the most pleasing tone and pitch that you desire, and compare the other lugs to it. Listen to Track 10 to hear the different pitches at each lug point. Start with the lowest sounding lugs, and bring them up to your reference lug. Never tune down to a pitch. If you are too high, loosen the rod until it's below the desired pitch, and then bring it back up. Keep in mind that sometimes the lug that is actually low is the one directly across from the one you are tapping, and you'll need to bring that one up in pitch instead. Continue tapping the head near the lug you are tuning as you bring it up in pitch.

TRACK 11
Go back and forth between your reference lug and the one you are trying to match. As you begin to match the other lugs to your reference lug, realize that all of the changes you make will slightly affect your reference lug, too. As you get closer to reaching evenness in the head, you may find that you'll end up choosing a *different* reference lug. You will hear an example of this on Track 11.

A simple way to help you hear the pitch at each lug is to touch the middle of the head with one finger.

TRACK 12
Do not press hard, or it will raise the pitch of the head and defeat the purpose. This procedure controls overtones and clarifies the pitch, so you can better focus on each individual lug. Listen to Track 12 to hear the tapping at the different lugs—first without touching the head, then the more focused sound when touching the center of the head with one finger. This is a great way to tune the batter heads quickly when on a gig, without taking the drums off the mount or stand.

If you are installing clear heads, this tip that will help you *visually*. Position the drum you are tuning in such a way that you can see the reflection of a ceiling light off of the drumhead.

You will not only be able to hear, but now also see, any wavering differences between the lugs. Tap the head near the edge again, at the different lugs, to see the difference. The closer you are to getting the head in tune with itself, the slower the wavering. This is the same type of wavering effect experienced when tuning a guitar.

If at any point you feel that you are way off, you can always loosen all the tension rods all the way, and completely start over. Sometimes this is easier and less frustrating.

Every tom has a *most resonant frequency*. In other words, it will sound the fullest and most resonant at this certain point. You can tune higher or lower than this point, but it won't have this singing quality to the tone. If the drum is tuned to the shell's most resonating frequency, you should *feel* the low-end in your chest. Through practicing tuning and getting acquainted with your drums, when this point is reached, you will know it. It is generally found in the lower tuning range. Sit close to the drum while you are tuning, and get your head (and ear) close to the drumhead—you'll not only hear the subtle nuances, but also feel the low frequencies emanating from the shell. This is even more apparent in the larger toms.

Do this process on all of the resonate sides of your toms. Then flip them over, and repeat this entire procedure on the batter head sides.

Begin by working with your largest tom. While muting the batter head, tap the resonant head in the middle, and listen to the overall pitch of this head. Now mute the resonant head, and tap the batter head to compare the pitch to the resonate head. It is common practice to tune the two heads the same, or else the resonant head slightly higher than the batter. Fine-tune the heads according to your taste. Feel free to experiment with this. The tuning relationship of the batter and resonate heads has so much to do with the sound of your drums. In terms of physics, the rate at which the two heads vibrate together, or opposite one another, determines the length of that drum's sustain. In other words, if the heads are tuned close together, they will move, or vibrate, together for a longer duration when the batter head is struck. Conversely, if the heads are tuned quite a bit differently, the heads will more quickly cancel each other out. Tune the batter head for the pitch you desire, and the resonate head for sustain. If you tune the top and bottom heads to match, you'll get a clear and long sustain. If the bottom is slightly higher, you will get more projection and a livelier tone. By tuning the bottom head more loosely, you'll get less sustain, and a deeper, overall tone—more like a "thud." It's fine if you tune the two heads with a difference in pitch, but don't do this to the extreme.

TRACK 13

You will also notice pitch bend when tuning the batter and resonant heads differently; this will be most apparent in the lower tuning ranges. If the top and bottom heads are too different in pitch in relation to each other, the low-end sustain will come in late. In other words, there is a slight delay between the occurrence of the attack sound and the occurrence of the fullness of the sustain. But this "fullness" should happen immediately after the stick attack. Track 13 demonstrates this—first sounding late, then correctly.

TRACK 14

For a more of a "jazz" tuning, bring both heads up in pitch—quite a bit higher than the drum's most resonant tuning. Obviously, the tighter you make it, the less low-end you'll have; since not only is the pitch higher, but the sustain is also shorter, even if the top and bottom are tensioned the same. Listen to Track 14 to hear this jazz-type tuning. The higher you tune, the more "choked" the toms will sound. If that's the sound and feel you want, then tuning up is the way to go. Just remember to bring up the bottom head as much as the top. Feel free to experiment with tuning your toms at many different tension possibilities; but remember that both heads need to be fairly close in pitch (either the same, or with the resonant side slightly higher or lower). As you move between these different zones, note the differences in pitch, tone, attack, sustain, and the feel of the drum.

When testing the overall sound of the drum, hold it with one hand at the hoop, and hit the center of the batter head with a drumstick.

Make sure the entire drum is at least one foot off of the floor, or the sound of the bottom head may be restricted. If it is not the sound you desire, go back and fine-tune both heads. To listen to each individual head, mute the one you are not testing.

For some different head combinations and tunings, I've recorded the following tracks using my Noble & Cooley CD maple 9" x 12" tom with triple-flanged hoops. These should give you a good perspective on how both the type of head and tuning affect a drum's overall sound and characteristics.

TRACK 15

Track 15 uses a single-ply, medium, coated on top; and a single-ply, medium, clear on the bottom; tuned low.

TRACK 16

Track 16 uses the same heads as those used on Track 15, but tuned up a bit higher.

TRACK 17

Track 17 uses the same heads as those used on Track 15, but tuned quite high. This tuning is similar to a traditional jazz tuning.

TRACK 18

Track 18 uses a single-ply, thin, clear on top; and a single-ply, thin, clear on the bottom; tuned medium.

TRACK 19

Track 19 uses the same heads as those on Track 18, but tuned quite high. The thin heads respond more quickly, are more sensitive, and have a higher overall tone to them.

TRACK 20

Track 20 uses a double-ply, clear on top; and a single-ply, medium, clear on the bottom; tuned low.

TRACK 21

Track 21 uses the same heads as those used on Track 20, but tuned up a bit higher.

TRACK 22

Track 22 uses a double-ply, muffled-type, clear on top; and a single-ply, medium, clear on the bottom; tuned low.

TRACK 23

Track 23 uses the same heads as those used on Track 22, but tuned up a bit higher

Suspension Mounts

You may notice that, when held by the hoop, your drum resonates quite nicely when hit. But, when you attach it to the stand, it loses that wonderful sustain. A way to combat this problem is to add suspension mounts, such as RIMS. These days, most manufacturers of high-end drums use some sort of suspension mounts, and some mid-line drums have them as well. There are also after-market mounts that will fit any brand of drums, if you'd like to add them to your kit. Because the tom arm bracket is removed from the shell and attached through the tension rods to the suspension mount, the shell resonates freely—creating more sustain. If your floor tom uses legs, make sure the rubber feet haven't worn through. Believe it or not, the rubber feet will help the drum sustain longer. There are even special rubber feet available with a spring inside to help isolate the drum from the floor, for more sustain.

Tuning by Feel

Sometimes, after tuning by the procedures discussed, I will tune for feel. Maybe the batter head just feels too tight when played. For a deeper, "rock" tuning, I like to feel more of the stick going into the head. Try loosening the batter head just a little, and feel the difference. Keep in mind that you will again have to fine-tune at each lug, and will possibly have to re-adjust the resonant head to work with the new batter head tuning. Yes, this can take some time and practice, but in the end, you'll get to know your drums better—*and* they'll sound great. Even the type of hoops you have on your toms affect the feel of the drum. Triple-flanged hoops (those most commonly used) tend to feel spongy and produce more give to the head, so you can "lay" into it more. Die-cast hoops make the head feel more rigid, and drumsticks tend to bounce off of the head more easily, producing a more brittle quality when hit in the center.

Comparing the Toms Together

Once you've changed and tuned all of the tom heads, set them up and play them a little. Listen to the pitch intervals and sustain qualities between the different toms. They should sound similar in their respective pitches. If two drums are too close in pitch, you'll have to go back and either raise or lower one until they sound good together. The more toms you use, the closer in pitch to each other they need to be. Also, ask yourself if all of the toms seem to sustain in relation to each other. If not, go back and fine-tune the culprit to match the others.

TRACK 24

If your toms resonate a lot (especially when using single-ply heads), make sure the tuning between them results in pleasing and comparable intervals. The tuning of each tom may sound great when played by itself, away from the kit; but when set up together, they may display some dissonance between them. This dissonant sound is caused when you hit one tom, and the adjacent tom head also rings. This can be tricky to fix, but getting your toms to "sing" in harmony is well worth the effort. Listen to Track 24 to hear the dissonance, and then how they "fit" together after being tuned to harmonize.

After playing for a short while with new heads, you may notice that some or all of the heads may have dropped in pitch. This is due to the initial stretching and settling of the heads; you may have to go back and fine-tune them again. I actually prefer the sound of the heads after they've been played on for fifteen minutes or so. To me, after this short break-in period, they begin to "melt" together as a kit and lose some initial harshness.

Now it's time to work on the most signature drum on the kit. It is audibly the most recognizable drum. Not surprisingly, it happens to be the hardest drum on the set to tune (or at least the hardest to make sound good). The snare drum's most important, yet overlooked, parts—which create its signature sound—are the bottom head and the actual snares (the spiraled wires that touch the bottom head).

Snare drums are fascinating to me. They come in so many depths, diameters, and shell materials, with different quantities of lugs and types of hoops, that I just can't seem to own enough of them. They typically range in diameter from ten to fifteen inches—fourteen being the most standard—but twelve and thirteen-inch diameters are quickly becoming popular as main snares. Depths range from three to five inches for piccolo snares, five to five and one-half inches for standard sized snares, and six to eight inches for deep snares. With this many size options, you can see the many variations that are available today.

It's very common to own more than one snare drum. When playing live, it's quite useful to carry around an extra snare drum (or at lease a replacement drumhead) as a spare, in case you break a head. Many drummers even use two snare drums in their set-up—one in the normal position, and either a smaller or just different-sounding snare to the left of the hi-hat. Studio session drummers may take as few as two, or possibly as many as twenty snares to a session—not because of breaking heads, but to find the sound best suited for each song being recorded.

The Tuning Process

As with the toms, remove the snare drum from the stand, and begin by inspecting the snare side (bottom) head. If the snare side head is dented or torn in any way, you will need to replace it. Check for holes in the head by releasing the snare throw-off, and inspect the head at the ends of the snares where they come in contact with the head. If the head has no holes or cuts, but has been on for a long time, you may want to replace it anyway, due to any stretching and loss of tone.

Begin with the snare side up. Either place the drum on a table with a towel underneath, or on a carpeted floor to mute the head you are not working on. Notice how the snares are attached to the strainer and butt-side before disassembling.

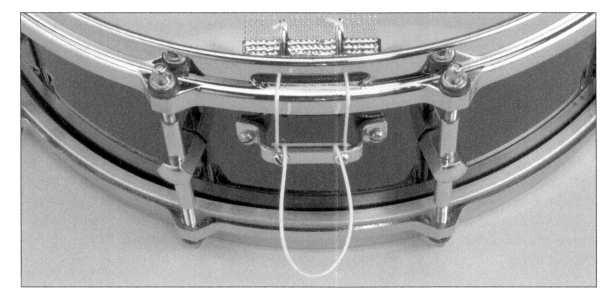

Examples of snare strainers attached with thread cord

Most snares can be attached to the snare strainer and butt-side using plastic straps, nylon cord, or plastic coated steel cable. Some strainers will not accommodate plastic straps, since they have holes through which you can only thread cord. Don't use shoestrings or leather straps, as they'll stretch and not hold a constant tension. The plastic straps are the easiest to install, but nylon cord and steel cable are better for finely positioning the snares for lateral adjustment. Here's a tip for reusing worn-out, single-ply drumheads: cut your own plastic straps from them. They need to be about eight inches long and one-half inch wide. If nothing else, cut some for spares to throw in your gig toolbox.

Remove the snares from the strainer and butt side. Some will require a drum key for loosening the screws, and others will take a standard or Phillips screwdriver. Inspect the snares for any that may be broken, missing, stretched more than others, or bent—and replace them. Snares come in all different types, and are made by many different manufacturers. Most are made of steel, but some are made of stainless and bronze. A typical, 20-strand, steel set of snares will set you back between ten and twenty dollars. Twenty-strands are the most popular, middle-of-the-road snares. However, if you'd prefer more of a "wet," full, snare sound, you may want to try up to a 42-strand set.

As described earlier, snare drums use an extremely thin resonant head, which works in conjunction with the snares. If you are a light player, use a thinner snare side head for increased sensitivity. Use a thicker snare side head if you are a heavy player.

Remove the snare side head and hoop from the snare drum, just as you did with the toms. Remember to use small increments on the tension rods when loosening, to avoid uneven stress on the shell and lugs. Notice that the bearing edge of the shell has two lower dips directly across from each other.

These dips are called *snare beds*, and are where the snares lay across the head. They are lower than the rest of the bearing edge to allow the snares better contact with the head. Since they are so important to the sound and sensitivity of the drum, some high-end snare manufacturers actually hand-cut the snare beds to insure their precision.

Clean the inside of the drum, and lube and tighten the lugs, if necessary, as you did with the toms. Place the new head on the drum, and spin it to see if it binds anywhere. If not, line up the head logo with the name badge on the shell. Clean the hoop, and place it on the new head already on the drum. Be sure to place the hoop correctly, so that the slots in the hoop (where the snares go) line up with the snare strainer and butt-side. Bring the snare side head up in tension, just as you did with the toms.

When fine-tuning, do not tap hard with a drumstick. You could tap with just your finger, or even lightly with the drum key. Because the head is so thin, it dents easily, and should never be hit other than a light tapping when tuning. Get the lugs as close to being in tune with each other as possible. Keep in mind that the lugs closest to the snare beds will naturally be slightly lower in pitch, because the snare beds are lower than the rest of the edge. In fact, once you are finished tuning, you may get a lot of "snare buzz" when playing certain toms, or when the kit is set up next to the bass player's amp. If you do, try loosening the four lugs closest to the snares a little bit, to reduce the buzz. If that doesn't do the trick, you may have to slightly change the tuning of the offending tom. You will never completely eliminate all of the buzzing; but a little is acceptable, since, for the most part, only you will hear it.

Now install the snares onto the drum using either snare cord or plastic straps. Make sure the correct side of the snares comes in contact with the head. Each end of the snares is soldered to where the snare cord or straps connect. This is the side that should make contact with the head.

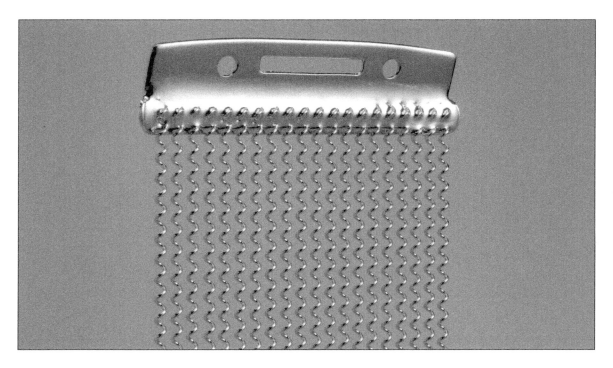

Ultimately, you'll want the snares centered at an equal distance from the edge of the drum. Begin by attaching the snare to the butt-side first. You may want to start with the snares just slightly closer to the butt-side, so that when you activate them later, they will pull towards the strainer and be even. Hold them securely in place with one hand as you feed the straps or cord through the butt-side holder, and slightly tighten down the screws to create a little friction, and make any final adjustments before completely tightening them down. Loosen the snare tension knob on the strainer so that it is extended fully (almost completely loose). As the snares stretch over time, you will have the maximum amount of adjustment. With the throw-off lever disengaged, feed the straps or cord through the strainer side, and tighten the screws again—just enough to create a little friction. As you engage the strainer, the straps or cord will slide into the correct position. Disengage the throw-off lever again, and tighten the screws completely. As you engage the snare strainer, look closely at the snares to see if they are pulling straight and evenly on both sides. If not, you'll have to loosen and re-adjust them. Check the individual snares by very lightly strumming your finger across them to determine if they are tensioned evenly. Unevenly tensioned snares is one of the main causes of snare buzz when hitting the toms, so spend some time to get it right.

If you'd like to do any additional fine-tuning of the snare side head, you can use a drumstick to create a bridge. Place the stick perpendicular to and between the snares and the drumhead with each end on opposite sides of the hoop.

This will allow you to tap the head without causing any snare buzz. We will come back to adjusting the snare tension and the snare side head after installing the new batter head.

TRACK 25

Flip the snare drum over so that the batter head is now facing up. Remove the head and hoop as before, and do any maintenance. Place the new head on, and tighten it one-half turn at a time (as you did with the toms), until you reach the desired pitch. At this point, you should be tuning the drum with the snare throw-off disengaged. Fine-tune the drum as needed, but here's another tip: when you feel you are very close to getting the head in tune with itself, play a rim shot (hit the drumhead with the tip, and hit the hoop with the front one-third of the stick), off-center on the drum head. Listen to Track 25 to hear an off-center rim shot. You don't need to play the rim shot near any particular lug, since you are listening to the overall batter head sound. The rim shot will help you to hear any wavering from out-of-tune lugs. Still tap at each lug to find the low or high spots; but occasionally, play the rim shot to hear if the wavering sound of the head smoothes out as you come closer to an even tuning. In fact, you can even hit the rim shot and tune up the low-sounding lug immediately. You will hear the wavering slow down as you tighten the lug to match the others. Listen to Track 26 to hear this snare get fine-tuned. Snare drums are generally tuned higher than toms, and will have a shorter sustain due to the higher tuning, but will produce more of a pitch the higher you tune.

TRACK 26

Place the snare drum on the stand, being careful not to poke through the bottom head with the snare stand basket, and engage the snare throw-off. Hit the drum in the center, as you would normally play, and just listen. At this point, you may still be quite a ways off from the drum sounding really good, but not for long.

Remove the snare from the stand while you are sitting on your drum stool, and flip the drum onto your lap, so that the batter head is facing your chest.

You should now be able to see the bottom head. The snares should be horizontal. Take your index finger and press the snare side head close to the middle, but right next to the snares. As you push in, view the reflection of the snares in the drumhead.

For a fairly standard, all-around tension, I recommend that the reflection span about three inches on a 14" diameter snare drum. If the head is too loose, you may see up to seven inches in the reflection; and when you play the drum, you'll hear a sort of slap-back sound from the head and snares. If it is too loose, tighten the lugs and view it again. Then put it on the stand, hit it again, and listen. When the snare side head is tighter, the sound will be more focused, and the snares will be more sensitive. Just don't tighten it too much, or you'll choke the drum.

Adjusting the Snare Tension

Adjusting the snare tension is a tuning practice often overlooked by inexperienced drummers. Some drummers believe it's either on or off, but the sweetest part of tuning a snare drum is getting the snare tension to work with the snare side head tension.

TRACK 27

TRACK 28

TRACK 29

Adjust the snare tension using the knob on the strainer. Always adjust this with the throw-off in the off position; then turn it on again, and test the drum by hitting the batter head. As you begin to tighten the snare side head, the looser the snares will sound, and you'll need to adjust them accordingly. Tensioning the snares is also a personal thing. To test the snare sensitivity, have the snares on, play very softly in the center of the batter head, and listen. If they tend to rattle too much, you'll need to tighten them up. Track 27 demonstrates snares that are too loose. If your snare drum sounds too tom-like or choked, the snares may be too tight. For a choked snare example, listen to Track 28. As in the audio example on Track 29, the snares should sound good when hit very softly or very hard.

Some drummers adjust their drum's snare tension to fit the style of music they are playing. As an example, blues drummers might want the snares a little looser to sound "fatter," and a pop drummer might want them tighter and more articulate. Just use your best judgment, and don't tighten or loosen the snares to the extremes.

If you are a light hitter, you can have a fairly medium tension on the snare side head. The harder you play, the tighter you'll need to make the snare side head. When you hit the snare drum batter head, it forces a column of air down towards the snare side head. If the snare side head is loose, and you hit the batter head hard, the snare side head moves a greater distance than it would when tighter. Keep in mind that the snares will also be forced to stretch along with the head. If they do, the drum will then sound less articulate and sloppier. Once you've adjusted the snares, you should be there!

Muffling the Snare Drum

Some drummers may choose to dampen their snare drum batter head to reduce some overtones. Never tune your drums when using muffling. Tune them wide open, and then muffle to taste, if desired at all. Some different options for muffling include: plastic rings, Moongel, external clip-on dampeners, and duct (gaffers or stage) tape. As I mentioned before, I prefer not to use any type of internal, built-in mufflers. They press up on the underside of the batter head, and throw it out of tune. When you hit the batter head, it presses even harder against the muffler. They also tend to rattle, and sometimes lose parts that end up bouncing around inside the drum when played. All of the other types of external muffling work great. Moongel is my favorite, since you can move it around to adjust the overall dampening, and it can be used with any drum size. The plastic rings work quite well, too. Be careful not to bend them, or they won't sit flat on the head, and may buzz. Rings are made by a few different manufacturers, and come in different widths and sizes to fit your toms. You can also make some yourself using old single-ply drumheads. Take an old head that matches the size of the drum you want to muffle. You'll want to carefully cut out the head, right where it flattens out past the collar, and discard the metal ring part of the drumhead. Depending on how much muffling you'd like, measure inwards about three inches from the edge, and cut out the center. You will now have a dampening ring. Place it on your snare (or tom) to test it. If you'd prefer to muffle less, cut more off from the *inside* of the ring. You could make a bunch to have a selection of different widths (3/4", 1", 1 1/2", 2", etc.). External clip-on dampeners also work quite well. Duct tape works, too, in a bind, but isn't as easily adjustable, and leaves a sticky residue when removed.

Keeping the Drum in Tune

Drumheads do stretch, although they do so mostly within the first few hours of playing (then they begin to wear out where hit). Often, it is easy to mistake the head stretching for the detuning effect. But in reality, the tension rods loosen up from vibrations when the drum is played. There have been several products designed to help prevent this problem. One of these is a nut that threads on the tension rod before you thread it into the lug. Once the drum is tuned, you would spin this nut down onto the lug, which helps to hold it in place. Index Tension Tuners are replacement tension rods that use miniature ball bearings to create clicks as you turn them, which help to keep the rods from backing out. Lug Locks are my favorite, since they seem to work the best for me. Lug Locks consist of a piece of plastic with a hole, which you press down over the head of the tension rod. The hole forms to the shape of the rod. If the rod begins to back out, the Lug Lock hits the hoop of the drum to stop it.

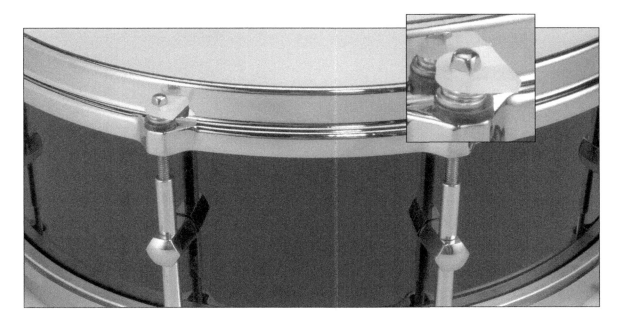

You can use any of these different products on your toms and snares. Typically, the snare drum will need it the most. I install Lug Locks on my snare drum batter side, on the four lugs closest to me—in other words, where the sticks come in contact with the hoop during rim shots.

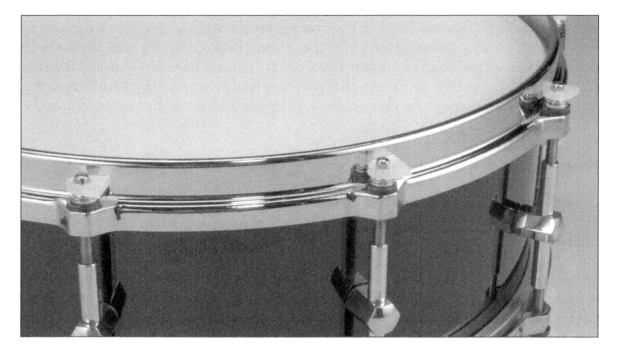

Sometimes during hard playing, the snare side (bottom) tension rod closest to where I play rim shots loosens up and falls out of the hoop—if I haven't also put a Lug Lock there.

All in all, these are a few great ways to help keep your drums in tune.

The bass drum is quite important to the overall sound of the drum set. If provides the pulsating thump that makes people tap their feet. It is often the most muffled drum on the kit, unless the more open "jazz" sound of the smaller bass drums is preferred. Because it is hit in the same place every time, it is the most consistent-sounding drum.

Bass drums typically range in size from eighteen to twenty-four inches in diameter, but even larger bass drums are available through some manufacturers. The most standard diameter was, and still is, twenty-two inches; but bass drum depths have changed over the years—the original standard being fourteen inches, then increasing to sixteen, and is now, typically, eighteen.

The Tuning Process

To begin, remove the bass drum from your drum set-up, and place it on the floor with the batter head facing up. Remove the batter head by loosening the tension rods as you did with the snare and toms. Bass drums will come with either T-rods, which you can turn with your hands, or the regular-type rods—as found on snares and toms, which require a drum key.

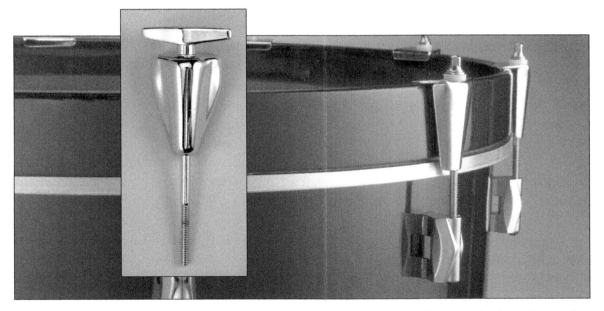

Both the T-rods and the regular rods work mechanically well enough, but those that require a drum key work best when using cases (the "Ts" can get caught on the case's interior foam). Once all of the tension rods are completely removed from the lugs, pull the head and hoop from the shell. Again, it's easiest to just let the tension rods dangle from the hoop, as you set the whole works down on your drum stool. Most bass drums have claws that attach the tension rods to the hoop. Because the rods just hook over the hoop, be careful when pulling everything off of the drum, to ensure that rods don't slide around on the hoop. If your bass drum hoops are made of wood, as they are on many high-end drums, the claws may have left indentations at the spots where they hook over the hoop. When you put the head back on the drum, you may want to try to hide these marks by keeping the claws in the same place on the hoop.

Since the head is now off, do the routine maintenance (tighten and lube the lugs, check the bearing edge, and remove any dust inside the shell) before installing the new head. Place the new head on the shell and replace the hoop. Align the hoop just as it was before you removed it, so that the pedal connects at the same place. Carefully guide the hanging tension rods around the head. Hold the claw with one hand to keep it steady on the hoop, thread the tension rod into the lug, and finger-tighten as you did on the toms and snare. Tension the head in one-half turn increments. After you've gone around twice, place your hands in the center of the head to seat it. Test the drum's tone. If it sounds too high, and you are going for a very low tuning, you might have to back out the tension rods, and bring them up to the desired pitch. When playing the batter head, you may also want to adjust the head for *feel*. If it's tight, you'll have much more rebound off of the head; while with loose tuning, you can play more "into" the head, with less rebound. Fine-tune the head by tapping near each lug. High tunings allow the drum to resonate longer, and are sometimes used by jazz drummers on smaller (such as eighteen-inch diameter) bass drums. This form of tuning is more similar to that of a tom-tom.

Although most drumhead manufacturers offer bass drum heads with built-in muffling, you may still wish to use some additional dampening inside the shell. Examples of additional dampening are pillows, towels, foam, felt strips (for use between the head and bearing edge), insulation, packing peanuts, shredded newspaper, and specially manufactured bass drum pillows. These different types of muffling range greatly in price, but many of them may already be lying around your house. Because the bass drum is muffled on the inside, you may end up having to remove the head, insert different muffling, and reinstall the head a few times until you find a sound you like. I prefer the manufactured bass drum pillows for bass drums that will be moved around a lot, since they adhere to the drum with Velcro, and won't move when the drum is flipped upside down in the case. The design of these pillows also enables you to use more than one: either doubled-up on the batter side, or placed on each the batter and resonant sides.

With a muffling type chosen, you can move on to the resonant head. Flip the bass drum over so that the resonant head is facing up; remove the old head, and do the routine maintenance. Place the new head on the drum; if it has a brand name logo, make sure that it is centered on the drum. Finger-tighten the tension rods into the lugs, and tension up the head. If your bass drum head has a hole cut into it, be careful when tightening it up. I would suggest *not* seating it with your hands it if there is a hole. For the lowest pitch, tension the head just beyond finger-tight. Try to at least get the wrinkles out, or the tone quality and projection will be lost. Tap with your finger at each lug point to compare pitches. Hitting the head with a stick may leave marks on the head, which may not be desirable, since this is the head the audience will see. If you'd like more sustain, tighten the resonant head up a turn or so.

A hole cut into the resonant head usually has two purposes. The first is to allow for a microphone to be placed inside the drum—either for recording, or for amplification through a live performance sound system. In live performance, when using a microphone on a stand in front of your bass drum, be careful to place it so that your guitarist or singer doesn't accidentally kick it and tear the head (which they're notorious for doing). The second purpose of the hole is to let the air escape from inside the drum. When you use a full front head, the air can't escape, except through the small air vent in the shell. When playing with a full front head, you may experience the pedal beater bouncing back off of the batter head. If your technique is to "bury the beater," you might find this set-up frustrating. You could try loosening the batter head until it almost wrinkles, or you could cut a small hole in the resonant head to allow the air to escape. To still get a sound similar to that of a full front head, cut a five-inch hole, off-center, about two and one-half inches from the edge.

If you cut a hole in the middle, or one larger than about six inches, you will lose the sound and resonance of the front head completely. There is nothing wrong with this, if this is the sound you are looking for. Remember: the larger the hole, the more attack, and the less tone and resonance. Also, the larger the hole, the less beater rebound you'll get off the batter head.

Making a Hole in the Resonant Head

Many drumhead manufacturers offer resonant heads with pre-cut holes as part of their product line. If you'd prefer not to spend the extra money, and cut the full head you've got, here are a few tips. Find something with which to trace the hole on the head—a small splash cymbal, coffee can, CD, or anything else that is round and the appropriate size. Some manufacturers have pre-made templates for this, too. After determining where on the head you'd like the hole, use a felt-tip pen to trace the object on the inside of the head. Place the head on cardboard, or something else you can cut into (when the razor blade goes through the head, you don't want to cut your carpet or mom's new linoleum). With the razor blade, begin cutting out the hole. Take your time, and be very careful not to cut *outside* the line. If anything, cut in toward the center. If you slip and cut outward, the head may tear easily once you begin playing.

There is another trick for making a hole—one that definitely requires adult supervision, and I claim no responsibility for misuse. Find a coffee or some other type of can to match the size of the hole you'd like. Heat your stove burner on high, and place the empty can on the burner to heat it up. The bass drum head should be off of the drum, and placed on concrete—such as a garage floor or sidewalk—with the outside of the head facing up. Remove the heated can from the burner with pliers, and carefully lower it onto the head at the desired place. If the can is hot enough, it should melt a perfect hole through the head. Let the head cool for a few minutes before putting it on your bass drum.

Testing the Bass Drum

Now that both heads are on, and you've decided whether or not to use internal muffling, it's time to set up and try the drum. Clamp your pedal on the bass drum hoop. Adjust the spurs on the bass drum so that the front hoop is raised off of the floor. Raise the drum just enough to slide your fingers under the hoop; tighten the spurs, making sure they are even and the drum sits straight.

Setting the bass drum on carpet will help to prevent it from sliding forward when playing; so most spurs have retractable spikes for this use. Raising the front hoop off of the ground affects the feel of the bass drum, because the higher you raise the hoop, the shorter the distance between the batter head and the pedal beater. Adjust the beater height so that it hits close to the middle of the drum. The height of the beater also affects the feel of the pedal. If the beater is extended out as far as it will go, but you feel that the throw of the beater still needs more weight, you can purchase small weights that attach to the beater's shaft.

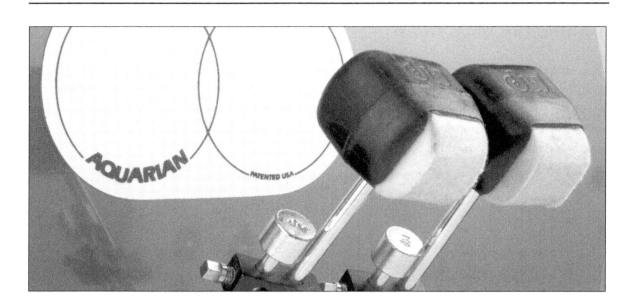

Once the bass drum is set up, listen to it from the audience's perspective (ten or more feet away), while a friend plays it. You can also attempt to do it yourself. Play the drum with your foot on the pedal, at the same time reaching your head around to the front to hear the resonant head.

This may seem sort of awkward, but it's the only way you'll be able to listen to the resonant head on your own. Make any final adjustments after playing the drum.

Bass Drum Batter Head Protection

Since the bass drum is hit consistently in the same place, you'll want to protect the head from wearing out prematurely. The heads will dent and wear out quickly; friction causes heat build-up, which will ultimately cause failure of the head. There is quite a range of materials used to make the protective patches. Some patches do alter the initial attack, but generally they add longevity to bass drum head. They usually come sized for use with a single pedal, but are also offered in a wider version to accommodate users of double pedals.

Some patches use a plastic or metal disc to accentuate the attack, or "click," of the hit. The type of patch you use should ultimately be determined by the style of music you play, and the sound you are shooting for. I prefer patches that are manufactured specifically for drum heads, but Moleskin Padding by Dr. Scholl's is a readily available, inexpensive alternative that can be purchased at a drugstore.

To install the patches, remove the adhesive backing from the patch and depress the pedal so that the beater almost comes in contact with the head. This is to make sure the beater will hit in the center of the patch, since not all beaters hit exactly in the center of the head. Once it's lined up, stick the patch onto the head, and you're ready to go! One more tip—don't use duct tape to protect the head from the beater. When the tape begins to wear through, its adhesive will stick to the beater head.

Bass Drum Beaters

In addition to the tone being altered by a patch, the type of bass drum beater you use can also have quite an effect on the sound. A softer, felt beater will sound much warmer and mellower than a wood or plastic beater, which adds more "click" to the sound. You may decide to have more than one to choose from, in order to alter your sound when recording. Some of the beaters available have as many as four different surfaces, which are accessible by just spinning the beater a quarter-turn.

Now that you have completely tuned your entire drum set, it's time to listen to it as a whole. Your drums may sound great individually, but how do they sound together? Put your kit back together, with cymbals and everything. Sit down and play for a few minutes. Listen to how the toms sound with the bass drum and snare. Do they fit in with the same genre of music, or are the toms tuned high for jazz, and the bass and snare tuned deep and rock-like? Do the individual toms sound like they belong together collectively as a group? They should have a similar tone and resonance to them. Do the pitch intervals between the toms sound good, or are two of the toms tuned too close together? You may have to go back and retune some drums until they fit with the kit as a whole. As with a guitar, the strings sound (other than pitch) as a group—their tone and volume are quite consistently even. The modern drum set is made up of many separate instruments, but you must always think of the sounds coming from them as a whole. Better drummers tend to play each drum at a volume that relates to the other drums, so that the kit sounds consistent and more like one cohesive instrument.

There are few manufacturers that offer products designed to aid the tuning process. Be aware that no tuning aid device can serve as a replacement for the human ear. Having said that, these products are helpful for getting close, and are a great learning tool for someone inexperienced with tuning drums.

There are two types of tuning aid devices. The first, used on the tension rod when tightening, is set for a desired level of tension resistance. Depending on the brand, the device will indicate when the set tension level has been reached, either on a meter, or by "clicking" into place. Although both brands measure the resistance required to tension up each rod, the fact that some tension rods turn harder than others can be a problem; obviously, this factor will affect the "reading" when trying to tune the drum.

The second type of aid is one placed directly on the drumhead. It can measure the tension of the drumhead either at the different lug points, or in the center for an overall reading on the dial.

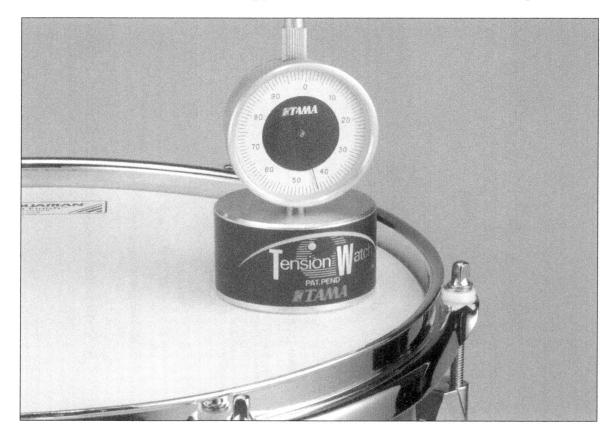

These devices are helpful when trying to match the tension at each lug; but you need to pick them up and set them down a few times to take an average reading, since the reading fluctuates each time you do. It's a good idea to write down the tension measurements for all of your drums once you get them sounding the way you want. These tuning devices also work well at gigs, where you may need to change heads quietly before show time, and want to quickly get pretty close. Anytime I've ever used one of these devices, I've still always fine-tuned by ear; so don't use them as a replacement, but instead as a guide.

DRUM SOUNDS AND TUNING OVER THE YEARS

Drum sounds and tuning have changed quite a bit over the years. This is due to the actual construction of the drums themselves, as well as changing styles and trends.

In my opinion, the better the recording technology, the more tuning precision necessary. Many early records were recorded using one or two microphones for the whole band! The "mix" was dependant on where the musicians were placed in the room. If the drums were too loud, the engineer would just move them farther back, away from the mic(s). Today (and since the invention of multi-track recording by Les Paul in the late 1940s), drums are even more "under the microscope," as it is now a common recording practice to set up one close-range microphone per drumhead. You can see how picky we drummers now need to be.

Years ago, drums used calfskin drumheads. Calfskin heads produced an appealing, warm tone, but were extremely affected by the weather (on hot, moist days they felt sluggish, on cold days they felt brittle). In the late 1950s, Mylar heads were developed to combat these problems. They were more durable and unaffected by the weather.

Sometime around the mid '50s, rock 'n' roll was born. Many of the drummers came out of the jazz/big band era, so their tuning was generally open and higher in pitch. The invention of double-ply and hydraulic heads in the early '70s allowed rock drummers to tune lower, and to produce a much more muffled tom sound. Many rock drummers also left their front bass drum heads off, and stuffed heavy blankets inside for a dry, "thud" sound. Many of the recordings representative of this time produced no room ambience at all, because the drums were recorded from dead-sounding drum booths. As the quality and techniques of recording began improve, the lower frequencies of low tuning were better reproduced.

Throughout the '70s and early '80s, concert toms were quite popular (many drummers created these by just removing the bottom heads on their double-headed toms). As discussed earlier, with the removal of the bottom heads, you get a dead, non-sustaining sound.

During the 1980s, drum construction continued to get better and more inventive—with better hardware and increasing shell thickness options. Deep tom sizes were the rage for rock drummers. Huge double bass kits with tons of toms became the norm. Drummers during this time were being recorded in larger, more ambient rooms, which resulted in bigger, more ambient drum sounds. But it was also a difficult time for the drummer in general, due to the increasing popularity of the drum machine. It was thought that, over time, these devices would eventually replace drummers. Thankfully, that didn't happen.

The late '80s brought in thinner, more resonant shell designs, even more head choices, and RIMS mounts to increase the drums' natural sustain.

In the '90s, smaller drum set-ups became desired again. Many drummers replaced their double bass drums with a double pedal. Many smaller, custom drum companies began to sprout up, flooding drummers with many new options to choose from. A new fast/quick tom depth became prevalent; again giving drummers more options. Some companies took it to the extreme, and made compact "travel" drum sets that would fold up into one case.

Today, the quality and selection of drums available to us are ever increasing. This is pretty amazing, since we're playing the world's oldest instrument (with the exception of the human voice).

WHEN TO CHANGE HEADS

When to change your drums' heads, of course, depends on your situation. If you are a student just learning to play, chances are the heads you are using (as long as they are not broken) are fine. If you are in a band that practices a lot and gigs occasionally, you might want to at least change your snare head before the gig, and maybe the tom batter heads if they are quite worn. If you play professionally—doing a lot of recording sessions and prestigious live shows—your standards may be quite a bit higher. It also depends on the type of music and how hard you play. Some warning signs include:

• Obviously, if the head is broken or torn in any way.

• If there are excessive dents in the head, or the white coating is worn through.

• If you are unable to tune the drum or get a full, clear tone. Worn-out tom heads will lack the low frequencies that are easily attainable with a new head.

• If, on snare and tom heads, you notice a variation in pitch in the center of the head (where hit), versus outside the general striking area. The feel tends to be "mushy" and dull, with a worsened stick response. When the head is removed from the drum, it will appear dished-out in the center, where it was hit continuously.

• You may just want to change heads to attain a different sound (such as changing from medium to double-ply heads).

- Always mute the head you are not working on by setting the drum on a carpeted floor or a towel, in order to get each head in tune with itself. Then, pick up the drum, and hit it to hear both heads working together.

- It's best to change all of your tom heads at the same time (at least the batter heads), so that they all produce the same richness of tone.

- Tune each drum to its optimal pitch. Each drum has a sweet spot where it sounds best. You can tune above or below this spot, but the drum sounds fullest at this pitch.

- On toms, tune the top head for pitch and feel, and the bottom head for sustain.

- Begin tuning your toms with the largest one first, so you can start at the lowest pitch and work up; then you won't have to tune the smallest tom way too high.

- Once you have all of your toms tuned individually, try them all together as a group to make sure that they sound good collectively. Make sure there is enough difference in pitch between each tom. The difficulty with this occurs when you are tuning a standard five-piece set (with tom sizes of 12", 13", and 16"), as it is hard to tune toms for much pitch difference when there is only a one-inch variance between them. If you are purchasing a new, high-end drum set, choose tom sizes that are at least two inches apart.

- Understand that the type of heads you select will determine, to a certain degree, how high or low you can tune. In other words, select the proper drumhead for the style you intend to play.

- Always tune the drums wide open, and muffle the heads once they're in tune, if you desire to do so at all.

- Drummers who are inexperienced at tuning often neglect to tune the resonant heads. Because they're not hit, drummers don't realize how significant these heads are to the overall sound of the drums.

- A typical cop-out for a poorly tuned drum is to use too much muffling to mask the drum's sound.

- Remember that when you put something on the head, it not only muffles the sound, it also dulls the high frequencies and slightly deepens the pitch of the drum.

- Always turn the drum key in small increments when tuning, so as not to pull the head unevenly to one side or the other.

- When fine-tuning a drum, the tendency is to find the low-sounding lugs and tune them up. Instead, if the head is too high in pitch for your taste, bring the high lugs back down. Just remember to de-tune the tension rod lower, and then bring it up to the new pitch.

- Always tune the drum you are working on away from your other drums, in order to hear that drum alone and more clearly. The other drums (and cymbals) will resonate when you hit the drum you are working on and cloud your pitch reference, making it more difficult to tune.

- Once you believe your whole kit is tuned up, have a friend play it while you stand a few yards in front of it and listen (however, take into consideration that your friend may play harder or softer than you). Then switch and get your friend's opinion.

- Whenever possible, tune your drums in an environment you are used to. You get used to how your drums sound and react when they are in a familiar place, such as your practice area.

- Carry at least one spare snare drum head, if not an extra snare drum to every session or gig, in case one breaks.

- Practice tuning for different styles using different heads. Experiment!

- If you are getting dents in your tom heads, you are either tuning too low, or your toms are angled too much, making you hit them incorrectly.

- Listen to the drums on your favorite recordings, and try to match your drums' sound and pitch to them. Also, try to match the snare tension and the amount of muffling.

- Talk to as many drummers as you can to find out how they tune, and to share ideas. It's always fun to hear what does and doesn't work for them. You don't have to reinvent the wheel. If you like their drum sound, ask them how they got it.

- Once you get your drums sounding the way you like them, use a drum tuning device that measures the drumhead's tension, and record on paper how high or low each head is tuned. You could also use an inexpensive tape recorder to record the pitch of each tom; then, when you change heads, you have a reference of how high or low each should be tuned.

- When attempting deep-sounding rock tuning, larger sticks will produce a fuller tone than light sticks.

- Tom-toms sound fullest when hit consistently in the center.

- For the most even and smoothest tuning, make sure that none of your drums are missing tension rods or washers.

- When browsing through your local drum shop, imagine how a particular drum set would sound before even hitting it, using the knowledge gained in this book. Remember, the size of the drums, their hoops, heads, bearing edges, types of wood, and many other things contribute to their overall sound. Then test the drums to see how close you were to your prediction.

- Before buying a new drum set, try tuning them to see if they are capable of sounding the way you'd like. You may even want to buy drumheads that you are used to, and try them on one of the toms.

- Use cases when transporting your drums, and do routine maintenance on them to keep your drums in top working order.

You have been exposed to quite a lot of information, and it may seem overwhelming at times. In its simplest conception, we are talking about no more than the stretching of a membrane over a cylinder—but you and I both know that there is much more to it than that. Take your time, and really practice tuning. The process can be difficult, but very personal and also rewarding when you play a finely tuned drum set. Nothing happens overnight, but you *will* gradually get better at tuning—if you follow the guidelines I've discussed. You may find it helpful to go back and review particular sections, or even the whole thing, to better understand the principles, techniques, and nuances of drum tuning.

ABOUT THE AUTHOR

Scott Schroedl is a full-time musician, performer, freelance studio player, and popular private-lesson music instructor based in Madison, Wisconsin. He is a published author whose previously released titles include the Hal Leonard *Sound Library Series* (three book/CD/CD-ROM packages of drum loops for use with music looping programs) and *Play Drums Today! Levels 1 and 2* (a self-teaching drum set method). In addition, Scott is a professional transcriber for both Hal Leonard Corporation and Cherry Lane Music, for whom he is also a prolific session drummer, having recorded well over 100 of the audio CDs that supplement their instructional books.

Scott proudly endorses Aquarian Drumheads, Axis Pedals, Noble & Cooley Drums, Paiste Cymbals, and Vic Firth Drumsticks.

For more information, including a complete listing of published titles and book reviews, or to contact Scott, visit www.scottschroedl.com